Golden

JAIPUR, AGRA & DELHI

Copyright 2018 by Sam's Travel Guide - All rights reserved.

The contents of this book may not be reproduced, duplicated or transmitted without direct permission from the author.

Jaipur

Essential Travel Tips – all you NEED to know

Copyright 2018 by Sam's Travel Guide - All rights reserved.

The contents of this book may not be reproduced, duplicated or transmitted without direct permission from the author.

.Table of Contents

Chapter 1: Introduction 1

Chapter 2: Things to Know About Jaipur....................3

Chapter 3: Best Places to Visit in Jaipur....................7

Chapter 4: Things to Eat in Jaipur 13

Chapter 5: Things to Avoid in Jaipur........................ 19

Chapter 6: Travel Tips for Rajasthan 22

Chapter 7: Haunted Places in Jaipur........................ 25

Chapter 8: Best Restaurants in Jaipur 28

Chapter 9: Best Hotels in Jaipur................................32

Chapter 10: Conclusion.. 37

Chapter 1: Introduction

Picture Courtesy: Country Inn and Suites

Jaipur is the pink city of India. India is famous for its vibrant colors. The country, having a rich heritage, does not fail to create awe among the tourists visiting the place. The country, with a combination of mountains, jungles and seas, enjoys a position of the 'top must visit places for tourists' on any travel list created anywhere in the world. Rajasthan spontaneously adds up to the vibrant colors of the country and is a place which is very popular among tourists. Jaipur happens to be the capital city of the state of Rajasthan and enjoys a position of being one of the best heritage locations of the country. The history of Jaipur is newer compared to that of the other cities in Rajasthan, although Jaipur has its own history of creation which dates back to the 18th century, having Jai Singh II as its creator. The Jantar Mantar and the Amer Fort in Jaipur enjoys the position of being UNESCO world heritage sights. The city of Jaipur forms a tourist's 'Golden Triangle' along with the cities of Delhi and Agra.

The city of Jaipur is named after its creator Maharaja Jai Singh II, who happened to be a Kachchwaha Rajput. The city was initially divided into nine blocks after its creation and contained all the major buildings such as offices and other residential buildings. Gradually the city became inhabited by a large number of people and was turned pink under the reign of Sawai Ram Singh, in order to welcome the Prince of Wales. The large population of the city has made it the tenth most populous city in the country.

As we have mentioned earlier, Jaipur enjoys the position of being one of the most eminent tourist destinations in the country enjoying the seventh rank in the 2008 Conde Nast Traveller Readers Choice Survey and the first rank in the 2015 TripAdvisors Travellers Choice Awards for Destinatitions. The various attractions of the city such as Hawa Mahal, Nahargarh Fort, Birla Mandir, Jal Mahal, Amer Fort, etc have been eminent tourist locations. The lanes and bi lanes of the city have various stories to narrate to its silent listener, as the city has witnessed various changes in history. We will be providing you with a detailed guide to Jaipur, which will be fascinating and adventurous.

Chapter 2: Things to Know About Jaipur

Picture Courtesy: **Rajasthan Tour Packages**

Jaipur, the land of color

It is a well-known fact that Jaipur is the land of color. Similarly, there are other cities with these colored references as well. Just as Jaipur is famously referred to as the Pink City, Udaipur is India's White city, Jaisalmer is India's Golden city, and Jodhpur is India's Blue city! The grandeur of the city of Jaipur, with lots of lights and music, is its basic characteristic which you are going to fall in love with. Roam around on foot to witness the local culture, although for those who prefer to roam around in vehicles, the city has appropriate transport services to offer as well.

Not all sand

A common misconception prevailing within the tourists is the belief that Jaipur is mainly sandy. Even though a major portion of the land of the state of Rajasthan is covered in sand with the Thar Desert near Jaisalmer, there is no lack of greenery in the state. Most of the cities have profound greenery that contributes to India's biodiversity. Jaipur has its own beauty, which is mostly dry land. The land of Mand has such a magnificent dryness to offer, do not miss its offerings.

Serene and bucolic landscape

Rajasthan' is primarily known for non-urban lifestyle and has a great bucolic landscape that resembles a painter's canvas, especially in seasons like the monsoon when the contrast between the sky above and the land below paints a beautiful picture.

The cultural references

The people of Rajasthan do not have the word 'shy' in their dictionary. They are outgoing and can easily adapt to situations and conditions, even make new friends. They are quite open, which is reflected in their trucks that openly endorse sultry images of female Bollywood actors.

Love for the Golden Age

A trip to Jaipur will make you relive all the classics in Bollywood. Songs written by renowned writers, sung by legendary singers, and performed by wonderful actors are all a part of Rajasthan's present culture. This is evident in the songs played by on the radios by taxi drivers, truck drivers, and even the restaurants in Jaipur. Famous personalities such as the comedian Asrani have their origins in Rajasthan.

Hospitality

People in Jaipur are known for their friendly nature and the hospitality they offer to tourists. They welcome you to their place with respect and do not let you leave without a hearty meal. Even strangers are offered a glass of water. The hospitality of the people in Jaipur reflects their cultural upbringing and the lineage lies way back in the history of the hospitable Rajputs.

Values and ethics

The values of people from Jaipur are reflected in their culture as well as in their nature. They are strict followers of religion with their culture heavily influenced by it. The attire they wear, with women covering their face with a veil and the men wearing a turban on their head are all hallmarks of Rajasthani culture.

Places to visit

The history associated with Jaipur is immense and deep-rooted. Palaces that were home to the kingship of Jaipur are now sites of attraction for tourists like the Jal mahal.

Chapter 3: Best Places to Visit in Jaipur

Picture Courtesy: <u>SUJÁN Luxury Camps & Palaces</u>

The city of Jaipur happens to be one of the biggest cities of grandeur situated in India. The various forts and other picturesque locations within the city are the best attractions for the tourists visiting India, as well as the Indian tourists. Below we have provided a detailed guide, which might further be beneficial for you in terms of roaming around in the city.

The Amber Fort

We begin with the Amber Fort, or the Amer Fort, as it is popularly known. The fort is one of the most popular forts not only in Jaipur, but also in Rajasthan. Amber Fort or Amer Fort is situated in Amer, on the top of a hill. It's the main attraction of Jaipur city. The fort was constructed by red sandstone and marbles. Amer fort is popularly known as the

Amer palace. This palace was the residence of the Rajput Maharajahs. The fort was declared as a UNESCO world heritage site along with five forts of Rajasthan. The fort has a magnificent mirror work and a beautiful light and sound show takes place on a regular basis. A famous elephant ride up to its gate allows tourists to have a splendid view of the mahals and chowks of the fort.

The Nahargarh Fort

Situated at the edge of Aravalli range Nahargarh fort creates a strong defense for Jaipur city along with Amer fort and Jaigarh fort. The fort was built in 1734. The view of the city of Jaipur from the Nahargarh Fort charms the visitors. Another attraction of the Nahargarh fort is the biological park which is inside the fort. Many Bollywood films have been shot here. The beautiful view of sunset attracts a large number of tourists every day. The café situated inside the fort serves tourists with various drinks and snacks. The Nahargarh Fort happens to be a favorite picnic spot for the tourists.

Jaigarh Fort Jaipur

Built by Jai Singh II in 1726, Jaigarh Fort is situated at the Aravalli range. The excellent view of the Aravalli range and Amber fort down below can be seen from the Jaigarh fort. The museum inside the fort exhibits pictures of the royals of

Rajasthan, swords, guns etc. The fort is situated on a promontory which is known as "cheel ka tila". The design of the Jaigarh Fort is very similar to that of Amer Fort, and the fort is also known as the victory fort. A huge canon named the "Jaivana" is situated within the fort. It happenes to be the world's largest canon on wheels. Subterranean museums connect the Jaigarh Fort and the Amer Fort.

The Hawa Mahal

The Hawa Mahal happens to be one of the most popular tourist destinations in Jaipur. The picture of the the Hawa Mahal is famous and its image is prevalent within the minds of tourists who are planning to visit Jaipur. Lets take a closer look. A peculiar façade and five rows, each containing windows which are bizarre in shape happens to be the first look of the Hawa Mahal. The Hawa Mahal was built in the year 1799, and legend says that wind used to pass from the small windows of the Palace. Presently the windows of the palace are shut and sealed. Earlier the dwellers of the Hawa Mahal used to get a glorious view of the city of Jaipur. The famous architecture reminds us of the dep rooted cultural history of Jaipur. A tourist can get a magnificent and panoramic view of the city if they climb to the top of the terrace.

The Jantar Mantar Observatory

The basic meaning of the word "Jantar Mantar" is calculating instrument. The famous observatory in Jaipur was built by King Jai Singh II, between the years 1727 to 1734. The Jantar Mantar happens to be a crucial astronomical point of the city. The structures prevalent within the Jantar Mantar have their own astronomical functions each. The observatory contains fourteen different structures, measuring time, calculating eclipses, etc. The Samrat Yantra Sundial which is situated at a height of nearly 90 feet happens to be one of the principal attractions of the Jantar Mantar.

The Monkey Temple

The Monkey Temple is situated in a peaceful surrounding and is quite attractive. The temple area consists of a sacred pool of water attracting those who are seeking salvation. The Monkey Temple, situated within a complex of temples and its atmosphere are adventurous. Lots of monkeys bathe within the pools situated within the temple. The animals cause no harm to the visitors and maintain a friendly relation with them. A good amount of tourists visit the temple each day and the place is filled with tourists, but be aware from the local "baba"s or to be more specific "pseudo baba"s asking for money.

The Albert Hall Museum

The architecture of the museum is mainly Islamic and Neo Gothic in nature, giving the palatial building a blend of various cultures. The model of the museum has been inspired by the Victoria and Albert museum in London. The museum was inaugurated and opened to the public in the year 1887 and contains various priceless items such as the paintings of Kings, clothes, weapons, etc used by the kings. An ancient Egyptian mummy belonging to the Ptolemaic Dynasty is preserved within the museum. If you are planning a tour to Jaipur, then you must essentially visit the magnificent museum.

The Amrapali Museum

The Amrapali Museum in Jaipur is not very old and features a variety of rare and timeless items. The museum principally features various jewelry products which are absolutely unique in nature. The owner of the brand has portrayed all sorts of jewelry in the museum, starting from the date when they began their business. Silver anklets for horses and Parsi Necklaces with a hidden message are some of the unique items displayed here. The collection provides immense amusement to the visitors.

Bagru Village

The Bagru Village is located at a distance of nearly one hour towards the south-west of Jaipur. Tourists can avail a half day tour to Bagru. The village of Bagru is mainly dedicated to the block printing craft. Various artisans can be noticed in the village and you can also see them in action. Tourists can see fabric drying in the. If the tourists have interest for textiles and the traditional procedures of block printing, then Bagru is their place.

Jaipur Zoo

Wildlife happens to be a principal issue throughout the world at present. With various rare species of life on earth slowly disappearing, Jaipur Zoo has created an exponent by preserving various forms of wildlife. A spectator will associate themselves with the beauty of wildlife once they visit the zoo. The history of the zoo dates back to the reign of Sawai Ram Singh II, who established it in the year 1877. Presently the zoo has an area of 33 acres. Various mammals and reptiles can be spotted inside the zoo. One can pot cheetahs, hyenas and colorful dears, along with a wide variety of birds. The peacock happens to attract a large amount of tourists. Spend some time within the wildlife, which leads to great refreshment.

Chapter 4: Things to Eat in Jaipur

Picture Courtesy: Quora

India is the land of cuisines, and each part of the country has its own unique delicacy. Rajasthan, having a rich culture altogether remembers to keep food imbibed in its cultural richness, and Jaipur enjoys a central position in terms of summing up the richness of delicacies in Rajasthan. Rajasthani food was inspired from a history of kings and warriors with creatively designed recipes and flavorful ingredients that were plentiful. Any trademark Rajasthani dish is packed with flavors that bring out an essence that only Rajasthani food can. We have mentioned below some of the popular delicacies of Jaipur, try them out.

Dal Bati Churma

This is Rajasthan's signature dish. It's famous among all tourists and the locals, who love to eat it for lunch or dinner. Baati, the bread, that requires least amount of water to cook, is eaten with lentil curry or dal. The " Dal" is generally prepared using Urhad Dal, Tuvad Dal, Mung Dal, etc. Various authentic spices are required in terms of making the dish. The locals of Jaipur love eating Dal Bati Churma, and it happens to be a staple diet of the people of the city. The Dal Bati Churma restaurant situated in Amer Road serves excellent quality of Dal Bati and is probably the best in Jaipur. Santosh Bhojonalaya situated in Dada Bari Road, also serves magnificent Dal Bati. Try out the local cuisine of Jaipur!

Gatte Ki Sabzi

As Rajasthan falls under a region where there is a constant lack of fresh water, a dish that doesn't require fresh vegetables would be one of their specialty. Gatte ki sabzi is one such dish, made from gram flour dumplings and a tomato-buttermilk gravy. Gatte happens to be cooked gram flower dumplings which are further added to a delicious gravy. Gatte Ki Sabzi is generally served along with Roti or any form of Indian flat bread. Shree Gopi Sabzi Walas located in the Sanganer Road Branch of Gopi Dhaba, serves one of the best Gatte Ki Sabzi. Veggies of Jaipur are not to be missed, as they are unique and innovative, especially simple concepts like Gatte Ki Sabzi turn out to be great with extreme innovation.

Laal Mans

For those who tend to think Jaipur is all vegan, think it again! Even with a majority of vegetarians in the Rajasthani population, their only non-vegetarian dish manages to impress most meat eaters. The dish uses red meat to cook a curry that has a trademark spicy sauce of green and red chilies. Rajwada Lal Maans serves one of the best quality Laal maans in Jaipur. Situated in Manosarovar Jaipur, this restaurant has attracted a good number of Non Veg lovers. The delicious mutton curry is irresistable. Try it out!

Ghevar

A dessert that is offered as a perfect culmination to every meal is the ghevar. Made from flour, this dessert's crunch packs a lot of sweetness. The nuts used in the ghevar add extra flavor when cooked with condensed milk. It is also available in different varieties. Ghevar is associated to the festivals of Teej and Rakhi, people of Jaipur celebrate the auspicious moment along with this sweet dish. For centuries, it has been a courtesy of the people of Jaipur to serve Ghevar to their guests.

Panchkuta

Comprising of five different, authentic ingredients that are available in plenitude in Jaipur , the panchkuta is an energizing and satisfying dish. The five key ingredients of the dish are Ker, Sangri, Kumat, gunda, and dry red chillies. The dish has been obtained from the dessert region of Rajasthan and is extremely simple and easy to make.

Papad Ki Sabzi

Papad Ki Sabzi (Rajasthani curry made from poppadoms), Jaipur.

'Eat what the locals eat, and you will never have a bad meal'. This mantra is religiously followed in Jaipur on all tours and travels .

People usually have Papad as an accompaniment, either as is, or jazzed up in the form of Masala Papads. The kitchens of Mewar however, found a lovely way to apply heat and bring out the flavors on an uncooked papad, in the form of a Sabzi !

So you may have a rather spicy, flavorful curry in which soaked, raw Papads are simmered. The Papads soak up all of that delicious broth and yet retain that quintessential spiced/bhuna flavor that is central to the experience. The Sabzi is wiped clean with some fresh phulkas and raw onions ! This dish is one of the most innovative Rajasthani dishes out there. With no vegetables required, the dish features roasted lentil flatbread that are cooked with yogurt to form a gravy that features chilli, turmeric, coriander, and the key ingredient of gram flour. The dish is very common to the locals of Jaipur.

Ker Sangri

One of the most popular Rajasthani dishes, Ker Sangri features two ingredients, Ker, a wild berry and Sangri, a long bean available widely across the state. These do not require a lot of water to cook and can be cooked well with oil or buttermilk. This made the dish a common feature among the locals. Both the rural and urban folks have Ker Sangri as their local cuisine.

Bajra Roti and Lahsun Chutney

Bajra is a common feature in almost all Rajasthani foods. Flat bread made from Bajra is usually eaten with a vegetable curry in every meal. Traditionally, Bajra roti is accompanied with Lahsun chutney, an intense garlic dip.

Raab

This is a dish that is made from the fermentation of millet flour and buttermilk. The thick broth is then cooked and served as a soup. Often, boiled corn kernels are added to the soup, then termed as 'makki ki raab'. It is an extremely popular local dish of Jaipur.

Payaz ki Kachauri

Onion kachori is enjoyed across Rajasthan as a snack that is eaten in the evenings. Plain flour breads are stuffed with a flavorful onion mixture. This is then fried for a little while and served hot with fresh coriander & mint chutney.

Chapter 5: Things to Avoid in Jaipur

Picture Courtesy: <u>Jaipur</u>

Packing Troubles

Jaipur's weather can be inconsistent. Even though the temperature is on the higher side mostly, it could get really cold in the winter here. It's always recommended to pack for both the heat as well as the cold. Enjoy the peculiar weather of dry Rajasthan.

Don't let locals manipulate you

Even though most of the people in Jaipur treat you as one of their own, don't let a travel guide lead you to shops owned by their friends or relatives. If they're claiming to get you cheaper deals, it's probable that they receive a commission for it and could mislead you.

Don't settle for more

The shopkeepers in Rajasthani markets are opportunists. They will not shy away from quoting a high price to tourists to make more profits. It is always recommended to bargain, and never agree to the first price offered by the shopkeeper.

Avoid street vendors

It is always better to go to stores with a government certification of authenticity, for genuine handicrafts and other products, since there is assured authenticity, which isn't the case with street vendors.

Safety around animals

Jaipur is famous for its wildlife sanctuaries and national parks, which is why certain etiquette needs to be maintained around them. Feeding animals, throwing things at them is dangerous. Elephant and Camel tours should be done under supervision.

Avoid superstitious gatherings

Jaipuri people are religious and fall prey to many superstitions. They perform acts of superstitions in public to draw attention to themselves. Avoid such gatherings as there are chances of getting physically hurt.

Avoid fake saints and priests

It is not advisable to take offers of spiritual advice and remedies from quacks, god men and saints, considering the fact that there is no way to distinguish the genuine ones from the crooks, who are just looking to trick you and make money.

Try to learn the language

Avoid relying only on your travel guides for communication. It also helps to know the language, so that strangers and shopkeepers don't try to take advantage of your unfamiliarity with the place and language.

Food specifications

The food that Jaipuris consume is usually spicy, hence it is important to explain your tastes and specifications to them. It is also safer to drink bottled water and eat well cooked food from a clean and hygienic place to avoid falling sick.

Chapter 6: Travel Tips for Rajasthan

Picture Courtesy: Mak

Jaipur is a state that is famous not only in the Asian continent but also across the globe for its culture and heritage. The authentic and colorful essence of Rajasthan is reflected in its markets, in its impressive dances, and the people who live to protect the culture. It is a hotspot for tourists across the world. This article specifically targets the people who travel to Rajasthan for a tour with ten tips for a good travel trip.

Travel Guide

Appointing a travel guide from a valid traveling agency will be extremely helpful. As the state has a deep-rooted and diverse history, you will not be able to cover it all and explore all the historic places that a tourist simply cannot miss!

Documents

As the case is with most travel trips, it is important to keep all your documents with you at all times to avoid any troubles. Documents for international visitors include Visa, Passports, and for local travelers, any other identification proof. This way, you can avoid having an inconvenient trip.

Accessorize

It is important to pack the right accessories for the trip. Especially for the shoes, you must consider carrying a pair of boots for the desert and a pair of flip flops for traveling in the city. Other accessories like sunglasses, hats, toiletries are essential on a trip.

Carry Indian Currency

The advantage of carrying Indian currency is the ease of transaction. You will not have to look for agencies and can easily avoid last minute problems especially during shopping in the city. By carrying local currency, you can also save an immense amount of money based on the exchange value.

Try to visit all attractions

Even though there is an abundance of palaces, forts, and historic places in Jaipiur, it is important to visit all these places of attractions to understand the depth of history and the roots of the culture of Rajasthan.

Read about Jaipur

To completely embrace and grab a complete picture of the rich culture and heritage of Jaipur, it is important to read about the state, its origin, its values, and ethics. Many books that serve as Travel guides to Jaipur are available.

Attend all city fairs

Jaipur is known across the world for it's Melas which attracts a large crowd with over a million attendees each year. These fairs are first on the list of every travel agency. A fair is a consortium of culture, food, people, shopping, and entertainment, all under one roof.

Shopping paradise

Rajasthan is a shopper's paradise! The handicrafts on display in the state fairs are elegantly designed with precision and expertise. The clothes like the colorful cholis, accessories like the hand-made jewelry, including art and crafts are renowned across the globe for their high quality.

Chapter 7: Haunted Places in Jaipur

Picture Courtesy: TravelTriangle

Jaipur's rich history of Royal lineages is popular across the world. This has managed to lure in two different kinds of tourists to Jaipur. The first being the history enthusiasts and the second, skeptics and believers, a minor group who are in search for spooky and mystic entities.

Kuldhara Village

The story of the haunted village of Kuldhara, Rajasthan is one among the strangest horror stories. The curse of an immortal minister, a local resident of Kuldhara is believed to be the reason behind the villagers migration to other lands for their habitation.

Brijraj Bhavan

Termed as 'The haunted mansion of Rajasthan', now a full-time heritage hotel is guarded by the ghost of Major Burton, an English soldier who resided here during the British Empire. He was killed along with his family at the Bhavan.

Bhangarh Fort

Regarded as the most haunted place in the country, the fort is famous among tourists and the locals. The haunted tales of the fort still send chills down the spine of each visitor. The fort is guarded by black magic performed by a tantrik who wanted to marry the queen.

Delhi Jaipur Highway

This is one of the most unique haunted places in Rajasthan as there is a dhaba(roadside eatery) that is said to be haunted by a female ghost. The dhaba on the Delhi-Jaipur highway was the location of an accident that killed a woman. Sources claim that a female ghost wearing a red saree is spotted near the dhaba.

The Nahargarh Fort

Located in a beautiful location lining the Aravalli hills, the Nahargarh fort has a view of the entire city of Jaipur. The fort was a home to the Royal family away from the noise and turmoils of the city. According to the locals, the ghost of Sawai Raja Man Singh guards this fort till date.

Jagatpura

Jagatpura happens to be a peaceful residential area in Jaipur. The place is believed to have been inflicted by witches who are believed to be haunting the city by night. The death of several villagers under the reign of a greedy kind has lead to the haunting atmosphere of the village. It takes real courage to roam around the city at night, as a woman in white saree is believed to stroll around the streets.

Chapter 8: Best Restaurants in Jaipur

Picture Courtesy: **Thrillophilia**

The Saba Haveli, Amer Road

The restaurant is located at a distance from the maddening crowds of the city and serves delicious and authentic Rajasthani cuisine. Tourists visiting Rajasthan fall in love with the restaurant. The menu of the restaurant is not pre decided and once the menu is set, items will be served only as per the menu. Diners can receive a magnificent view of the Nahargarh fort and the Garh Ganesh temple while having their meals. The architecture of the restaurant has a magnificent history and was created by a British architect nearly two hundred years back.

Spice Court, Civil Lines

The splendid outdoor seating arrangement of the restaurant attracts a large number of tourists and locals. The restaurant serves traditional delicacies such as Junglee Maas, Kima Bati, Laal Maas etc. The Junglee Maas cooked by the restaurant is a delight, as the ingredients happen to be ghee, red chilies, garlic and onion. Other dishes such as the Keema Churma and the Dal Bati are also tasty. A variety of vegan dishes su   ch as the Ker Sangri, Palak Korma and Spice court Aloo are also liked by the guests. The evening puppet shows organized by the restaurant are not to be missed as it happens to be an interesting local entertainment.

Swarn Mahal, Virasat Heritage Restaurant

The Swarn Mahal restaurant which is located in Virasat, has achieved immense success in maintaining the rich tradition of Rajasthani cuisine. The approach of the restaurant is sophisticated as they serve their guests in silver thalis and provide them with a royal treatment. The traditional and local thalis are not to be missed as you will not be able to receive the local flavors of Jaipur until and unless you taste their beautiful thalis. The restaurant authorities organize for local music and dance while the diners have their meals.

1135AD, Amer

The 1135AD, Amer has reached an exponential position by creating a distinct approach in terms of treating their guests. The approach of the restaurant is royal and will remind you of the rich cultural history of Rajasthan. The ten course thali of the restaurant is not to be missed as it reflects the artistry of Rajasthani cooking. The atmosphere of the restaurant is distinct and you as a tourist are sure to fall in love with the restaurant.

The Sury Mahal Restaurant, MI Road

The restaurant started as a mini fast food corner before its present position. The restaurant has progressed in leaps and bounds until it reached its present form. The restaurant has specialized in serving traditional dishes such as Gatte Ki Sabzi and other dishes such as the Masala Dosa, Dal Makhani, Black Dal and Desi Rajma. Not to forget that the restaurant began its journey as a fast food corner, therefore various food items such as Pao Bhaji, Sandwiches, and Chole Bhature are among the best cuisines of the restaurant. The magnificent thalis of the restaurant are loved by the locals and the customers who are loyal to them.

Handi, MI Road

The cuisines of Handi are not confined within the limits of Rajasthan. The restaurant serves various North Indian delights along with traditional Rajasthani cuisines. The various dishes such as the Tandoori Chicken and Chiken

Tikka served by the restaurant are delicious and loved by the tourists. Handi meat, which is slow cooked in a handi happen to be their signature delicacy. Other traditional Rajasthani dishes such as the Jungli Maas and the Laal Maas happen to be magnificent delights of this restaurant. The restaurant enjoys the topmost position in terms of serving non veg dishes in Jaipur.

Jungli Maas, Laal Maas, Chiken Tikka, Butter Chicken and Biriyani happens to be specialties of this restaurant. The restaurant has an outdoor sitting lunch arrangement which attracts various tourists.

Niros, MI Road.

The history of Niros dates back to a time period of the 1940s. The restaurant is said to be one of the primary introducers of Chinese in the city of Jaipur. Presently the restaurant has specialized in serving various North Indian delicacies along with their signature Chinese cuisines. Various dishes such as Jungli Maas, Laal Maas and Chicken Tikka happen to be the best. The Butter Chicken and Rogan josh are not to be missed.

Chapter 9: Best Hotels in Jaipur

Picture Courtesy: **Heritage Hotels of India**

Hotel Jal Mahal

Hotel Jal Mahal of Jaipur provides best facilities to their customers. This beautiful hotel has a garden inside. This 18th century palace was once Jaipur's Prime Ministerial palace. Now it is run by the Taj group. There is a gorgeous pool at the center of the hotel.

Information

Name- Jal Mahal Hotel

Address-Jacob Road , Civil Lines, Jaipur

Room rent-5000-7500 INR per night

Oberoi Rajvilas

The Oberoy Rajvilas is Situated 10 km away from Birla Mandir and 14 km from the island palace of Jal Mahal. This beautiful gorgeous hotel has sophisticated rooms, bars, restaurants and all modern facilities to make a perfect holiday. Oberoi hotels are famous for their warm hospitality in India and abroad and Rajvilas is not an exception to that.

Information

Name- The Oberoi Rajvilas

Address- Babaji Ka Modh, Goner Road, Jaipur 30203

Phone Number- 91 141 2680101

Email address- generalmanager.rajvilas@oberoihotels.com

The Raj Palace

The Raj Palace hotel is considered as one of world's best heritage hotels. This hotel has restaurants, bar, coffee shop, swimming pool, spa, and many other modern facilities.

Information

Name- The Raj Palace

Address- Jorawer Singh Gate, Amer road, Jaipur

Phone-91-1412634077/ 91-141-2634078

e-mail- gm@rajpalace.in, gkvhotel@gmail.com

The Pearl Palace Heritage Hotel

The Pearl Palace Heritage Hotel happens to stand in an extremely convenient location with major attractions such as Hawa Mahal and Amer Fort situated nearby. The Hotel offers magnificent non-smoking rooms with rooms packed up with beautiful artefacts. free wifi and parking space are also offered to the tourists. The beautiful seating area within the rooms leads to immense relaxation for the tourists. Each room within the hotel is air conditioned and has a flat screen TV.

Information

Distance from nearest airport- 7.4mi

Nearest Rail Station – Gopal Bari Railway Station.

Nearest Bus Station – Sindhi Bus Station

Shahpura House Hotel

The architecture of the hotel is a mixture of Mughal and Indian architecture. A ruling royal family of Jaipur has the hotel as their home. The hotel consists of various facilities such as free wifi, swimming pool, wellness center, etc. The bathrooms contain bathtubs and other facilities. One can enjoy to their hearts' content once in the hotel. The Rang Mahal restaurant situated within the hotel offers the guests with various cuisines, especially Rajasthani cuisine. Guests can enjoy magnificent views of the Amber Fort and Aravalli Hills. The Rang Mahal restaurant also provides its guests with various kinds of beverages.

Information

Nearest attractions- Jaigarh Fort, City Palace and Hawa Mahal.

Nearest Airport- Jaipur Airport.

The Royal Heritage Haveli

The building was constructed in the 18th century and happens to be one of the most magnificent hotels of Jaipur. The rich heritage of the hotel attracts a large number of tourists. The hotel provides its guests with facilities such as a swimming pool and free wifi. Guests thoroughly enjoy their stay in this magnificent hotel.

Information

Nearest attractions: Hawa Mahal, Jal Mahal.

Nearest Airport: Jaipur Airport.

Savista Retreat

The Savista Retreat happens to be a private mansion located in the peaceful country side. The various facilities provided by the hotel include a beautiful wellness centre with regular yoga lessons. The hotel contains private balconies for the guests. The magnificent architecture of the hotel has ensured to keep it among the top in terms of rankings in Jaipur.

Information

Nearest attraction – Amber Fort

Nearest Airport – Jaipur Airport.

Chapter 10: Conclusion

Picture Courtesy: JaipurCity Blog

The word Jaipur in India is associated not just with the popular state of Rajasthan but also with abstract emotions of happiness, a serene landscape filled with color, and culture. Many historical events are hidden in the city of Jaipur which helps tourists to recognize the history and culture of our nation from ancient age. Travelers from all over the world come here and satisfy themselves by witnessing the beautiful palaces and forts, magnificent beauty and breathtaking sceneries all around. Forts are present all around Jaipur, which carry along with themselves the mysteries of ancient history. Various historical events occurring within the forts have become lullabies presently. The city has a rich tradition of both folk and classical music. The famous Jaipur Gharana which was founded by Ustaad Alladiya Khan has taught pure Indian Classical music to a number of maestros in India.

Music lovers from all over India comes to pay homage to the glorious Jaipur Gharana in Jaipur. The delightful colors of India wait for you, so what are you waiting for, pack your bags and fly off!

Agra

Essential Travel Tips – all you NEED to know

Copyright 2018 by Sam's Travel Guide - All rights reserved.

The contents of this book may not be reproduced, duplicated or transmitted without direct permission from the author.

Table of Contents

CHAPTER 1: INTRODUCTION 41

CHAPTER 2: UNKNOWN FACTS ABOUT THE TAJ MAHAL 43

CHAPTER 3: TEN TIPS FOR TRAVELLING TO AGRA 50

CHAPTER4: INFORMATION FOR TRAVELLING AROUND AGRA 55

CHAPTER 5: FAMOUS ARCHITECTURAL WONDERS IN AGRA 59

CHAPTER 6: BEST RESTAURANTS IN AGRA 64

CHAPTER 7: MOST LUXURIOUS HOTELS IN AGRA 69

CHAPTER 8: THINGS TO AVOID IN AGRA 73

DON'T EVER TRUST A STRANGER 74

CHAPTER 9: BEST WEEKEND DESTINATIONS OF AGRA 77

CHAPTER 10: CONCLUSION 82

Chapter 1: Introduction

Picture Courtesy: Wikipedia

Agra, the city of Taj Mahal, is popular on a worldwide scale, attracting a large number of tourists from all parts of the globe. The city of Agra is located on the banks of River Yamuna, surrounded by cities such as Gwallior, Lucknow, Mathura and New Delhi. The city of Agra happens to be the most populous cities in UP and enjoys the position of being the 24th most populous city in India. The city of Agra happens to be a World Heritage Site, as stated by UNESCO. The various prestigious monuments located within the city such as the Agra Fort, Taj Mahal, Fatehpur Sikri, Sikandra, etc, enjoys immense popularity. Agra enjoys the position of being one of the major tourist triangles along with Jaipur and Delhi. The city of Agra, the history of which dates back to the Mahabharata, was previously known as Agrevana, as mentioned in the famous epic Mahabharata. It happened to be the capital city of the Mughal Empire. The city of Agra was later developed by a ruler of the Delhi Sultanate, Sikandar Lodi. His son Ibrahim Lodi maintained the glorious legacy until he was defeated in the Battle of Panipat. Agra was popular by the name of Akbarbad during the Mughal Empire, and happened to be significant both politically and culturally. Emperor Shah Jahan shifted the capital from Agra to Delhi before his son again shifted back the capital. The city received its name Agra under the rule of the Marathas after the Mughal rule.

Agra happens to be a magnificent city in terms of tourism, art and culture. The city resembles the cultural richness of India through its glorious monuments and stupendous atmosphere. Below we have mentioned the prime attractions of Agra. Life in Agra can be charming; you just have to gather proper information before your visit.

Chapter 2: Unknown Facts About the Taj Mahal

Picture Courtesy: Travel Genes

Taj Mahal, ever since its construction in the 16th century, has remained the center of attention. Known as the 'monument of love', there are several stories that revolve around the monument. While some of the stories are popularly known among people, there are a few untold, unknown things about the Taj Mahal that add to its historical significance. This article attempts to uncover the unknown facts of the Taj Mahal as well.

Time and Cost

There are many rumors surrounding the time taken for building the masterpiece that we now refer to as the Taj Mahal. The construction that began after the death of Begum Mumtaz, wife of Shahjahan, the Mughal emperor in 1632, took approximately 22 years to complete. By 1653, the Mahal was ready and had cost, what was then accounted for $32 million worth of resources, which comes to about $1 billion now.

Textures immanent within the glorious Taj Mahal are mainly Persian and Mughal with various scriptures inscribed on the building. Nearly a thousand elephants were involved with the construction of the Taj, and various precious materials used for the decoration of the Taj were bought from various places of the world, contributing to its immense beauty.

The man behind the scenes

Many may recognize and associate the Taj with Shah Jahan and his love for Mumtaz, but only a few know about the person behind the construction. Ustad Ahmad Lahauri was the chief architect involved in the construction of the monument. He was the sole person responsible for over 22,000 workers and a 1000 elephants. Mir Abd-Ul-Karim happened to be the second supervisor in the creation of Taj Mahal.

As per Ahmad Lahori, Shah Jahan took keen interest in art and architecture, and he would discuss about the progression and give Artistic advices to the chief supervisor on a regular basis. Ustad Ahmad Lahori was believed to be an Indo Persian architect.

The calligraphy of the building

With the Taj Mahal being a dedication and homage of Mumtaz Mahal, it has calligraphy all over the interior and exterior, which, among other patterns and holy inscriptions, also has calligraphy on the tomb that identifies and praises Mumtaz Mahal. Another interesting fact is that there are 99 names of Allah found on the sides of the actual tomb as calligraphic inscriptions. After all, Shah Jahan did envision Mumtaz's home in paradise, and Taj Mahal was that imagination coming to life.

There are holy inscriptions, mesmerizing patterns, and words of praise all over the Taj Mahal. The words all praise Mumtaz's beauty and the holy inscriptions are 99 names of Allah, an equivalent comparison to paradise for Mumtaz through the eyes of Shah Jahan.

The after effects

Taj Mahal, a symbol of eternal love.

It is located on the right bank of the Yamuna River in a vast Mughal garden that encompasses nearly 17 hectares, in the Agra District of Uttar Pradesh. The existence of several historical and Quranic inscriptions in Arabic script have facilitated setting the chronology of Taj Mahal. The Taj Mahal is considered to be the greatest architectural achievement in the whole range of Indo-Islamic architecture. Its architectural beauty has a rhythmic combination of solids and voids, concave and convex curves and light and shadow plays all over the structure. The colour combination of lush green and reddish pathway and blue sky over it show cases the monument in ever-changing tints and moods.

After the death of Mumtaz in 1631, Shah Jahan was devastated and within just a few months, the after effects began to show on his body. His hair turned white and the impact of the death was evident. Shah Jahan held Mumtaz very dear and regarded her as his most precious.

The (gem)stone

Made out of white marble, this beauty has red stone walls on three sides. The marble was ordered from different parts of India and beyond, the best in quality. The materials involved in erecting the monument cost a massive portion of the cost involved.

As we have mentioned earlier, precious items from all parts of the world were used in the creation of the Taj Mahal. Around 28 types of precious Gemstones were used in the creation of the Taj, along with marble and sandstone.

The colors of the Taj

If you thought the Taj Mahal was the color of pearls all through the day, you might want to rethink that. Changing colors with the time of the day, the Taj switches from a pinkish hue in the mornings to retaining its true color in the day, and turns bronze golden in moonlight.

As per many viewers, the changing colors of the Taj represent the changing moods of a woman. The bronze gold texture of the Taj can be captured in a full moon night, but be careful with the administrative measures. Taj Mahal at night is a long walk, and you cannot carry mobile phones along with you, so beware. Once you capture a view of the night time Taj, your heart can shatter down into pieces. Imagine an old and feeble Shah Jahan, craving for his symbol of love from his prison in the Agra Fort.

The Taj and its history of fire

The Taj Mahal was damaged during the rebellion of 1857. While the garden was harmed badly in the mishap, a few stones from the pillars were damaged in the process. The repair process for the Taj and the garden were ordered for by Lord Curzon. What we see today is the renovated structure.

The Geometry

The Taj Mahal is a symmetrical monument in almost every aspect. The monument forms a perfect mirror image in the pond right in front. However, the two tombs inside are not exactly equal. This intentional flaw by the architect was because he wanted the male tomb to be larger than the female tomb.

The myths about Taj Mahal

Among all the myths that surround the Taj, the one that is circulated the most is the myth about the workers. The Emperor Shah Jahan, in an attempt to prevent any further creation of a beauty like the Taj, had the thumbs of the workers chopped off. This isn't true and has no evidence to back it. Think about it, 22,000 workers, 44,000 severed thumbs! Not an auspicious inauguration.

Various stories of ghosts and mystery are not to be encouraged.

Echo for all eternity?

Even though the Taj Mahal is one of the most privileged sites to visit, a wonder of the world itself, it battles to remain glorious. With pollution all around and acid rains occurring frequently, the color of the Taj is turning yellow and with ash deposits, losing out on all its beauty.

Chapter 3: Ten Tips for Travelling to Agra

Picture Courtesy: Trident Hotels

The seventh wonder of the world, the monument of love, the pride of India, the Taj Mahal in Agra, Uttar Pradesh is a representative of almost every Indian tourism page. However, there is more to see than just the Taj Mahal in Agra, the city that hosts it. Here are some tips for a safe and rewarding trip to Agra.

Bear with the heat

Frequently visited by tourists, during the holiday season temperatures in Agra can touch 40 degrees. Even though the locals find it normal, tourists might find the weather uncomfortable for venturing out into the city. The heat wave is common during summer and it gets humid.

India, being a hot and humid country, will not be compromising with its heat during the months of summer. Stay prepared.

When to visit

The best time (season) to visit Agra is the winter season. During winters, extending from October to February, a cool breeze of fresh air accompanies your everyday adventures. The weather is pleasant, which makes sightseeing and monument hunts easier and adds to the city's memorable experience.

How to visit

As there is no direct flight to Agra, traveling from New Delhi via air is the fastest option. The Agra airport is a seasonal one that serves only the domestic Air India flights from New Delhi. You could also consider the trip to Agra through rail or road travel from major cities and tourist destinations in India.

Finding a place to stay

If you plan on staying for more than one day, booking a room in the hotels here is recommended. You can find hotels in abundance in the city in all three price ranges. Don't settle for accommodation, booking in advance at a mid-range or slightly expensive hotel will undoubtedly make your stay better.

Agra Darshan

Offered by the tourism department of the state government, the Agra Darshan is a guide to everything in the city worth visiting. The tour is available in both halfday and fullday options and are designed to not drill a hole in your wallet.

Photograph yourself

Even though there will be photographers who would be eager to photograph you, consider carrying your own camera. The price quoted by the photographers there is on the higher, impractical side for some sub-standard photographs. An average professional photographer will be charging you a sum of Rs. 800-1000, therefore it is better to photograph yourself.

Cab Vs Auto

Finding cab services in India, especially Agra is not as inconvenient as it was before. With cab services like Ola expanding their market, cabs while traveling in Agra offer best-in-class service in exchange for a slight increase in price.

Bargain till you drop

Sadar Bazaar in Agra, is a shopaholics' paradise that houses an array of handicraft items and leather products. It is the perfect place for you to find unique souvenirs, intricately designed to embellish your home. Being the local market in Agra, Sadar Bazaar is a place where you will find the best in leather and marble that Agra has to offer. Handicraft items including the famous Agra shoes are on offer. Bargaining will get you a reasonable offer for the beautiful items available in the market.

Plan your trip around the festival

There are several festivals that happen in Agra that take place throughout the course of the calendar year. Festivals such as the Taj Mahotsav and Taj Literature Festival, add to the tourist's attractions with events and festivities planned throughout the day.

Don't just visit the Taj

Agra isn't just about the Taj. The city has so much more to offer! You can explore other places such as Jama Masjid, Moti Masjid, Akbar's tomb, the river Yamuna, Agra fort and much more! Agra as a mark in history amazes me each time I travel. The city features on every Indian tour guide's itinerary and is a favorite among the locals as well as the tourists.

Chapter 4: Information for Travelling Around Agra

Picture Courtesy: Indian Holidays - Blogger

The major Historical attractions of Agra have been attracting tourists on a worldwide scale, but you always need to be careful and gather proper information before setting your foot on the streets of Agra. With proper information you can roam around the city with ease and zero difficulty.

Arriving and Leaving Agra

There are ample numbers of options in terms of arriving and leaving Agra, you can avail any one of them. In case of trains, there are two main rail stations in Agra, the principal of which is The Agra Fort Rail Station and then there is the Agra Cantt Railway Station The Agra Fort Railway station which lies at a distance of just a few kilometers from the Taj Mahal area will be convenient for you. The Agra Cantt Railway station lies at a distance of nearly 10 kilometers from the Taj Mahal. The station is well organized with proper platform numbers displayed on the screen. You as a tourist will not be having much difficulty in travelling to Agra from anywhere you like.

Places for staying in Agra

There are various types of hotels in Agra having a good range of economic aspects. You as a tourist can select your type as per your pocket. Hostels and Guest Houses also provide the tourists with accommodation; therefore you must know where to stay.

The Hotel Taj Plaza is situated at a distance of nearly 5 Km from the Taj Mahal. The hotel will provide you with a different view of the magnificent monument.

ITC Mughal Luxury Collection Hotel - The hotel is splendid with great food and luxury amenities, ideal for a tourist.

Hotel Atulya Raj - Great comfort and the breakfast of this hotel attract a large number of tourists, therefore you must consider this hotel.

Getting around Agra

Generally it is convenient for a tourist to find an accommodation near the Taj Mahal, preferably within a walking distance. Rickshaws and shuttles are the best possible modes of transport in Agra. The city happens to be hot and dusty, therefore, if you cannot bear with the immense heat, take a rickshaw to travel around. There are various types of rickshaws in Agra, the most of which are animal powered and also man powered. Autos are also convenient in case you want to avoid walking.

What to do in Agra

There are endless numbers of things to do in Agra. Visiting the historical monuments, shopping around the local bazars, tasting the best tastes of Agra are the common routines of the tourists visiting the city. You can definitely indulge into something interesting and unique, keep your eyes open and look around the fun and frolic waiting for you. The colorful bazars provide you with the best traditional cuisines of India, and also the best quality marble products.

Restaurants and food

Traditional Indian food along with a mixture of Mughal tastes waits for you in Agra, it is up to you to find the right place and indulge your taste buds. Various street foods along with kebabs and tikiyas happen to be the principal attractions of the city, check out, do not miss them.

Chapter 5: Famous Architectural Wonders in Agra

Picture Courstesy: Travel Tales

The Taj Mahal

This eternal symbol of love is counted as one of the Seven Wonders of the World, further attracting a large number of tourists. The mausoleum which was built of white marble has advanced geometric calculations used in its construction. An annual amount of nearly eight million tourists come to visit this beautiful monument. Special entry is allowed on the full moon nights in order to provide the tourists with a heart rendering view of this eternal monument. The monument is usually opened from 6am in the morning to 7am in the evening. UNESCO has granted the building with the title of a World Heritage Site.

The Agra Fort

The Agra Fort happens to be the best Mughal fort in India. The stupendous view of the Agra fort with a mixture of marble and red sand stone gives it a brilliant texture. The various contents of this magnificent fort, such as the Shisha Mahal, the Amar Singh Gate, happen to be the signature items of this Fort. The construction of the Agra Fort was started by emperor Akbar and was primarily an army base. Later the Fort was turned into a luxury fort by his son emperor Shah Jahan. A lot many tourists turn up to see the fort annually.

The Mehtab Bagh

The Mehtab Bagh is a magnificent garden built on the opposite side of the Taj Mahal. The Mehtab Bagh happens to be a "char bagh", or a four garden complex. The garden provides photographers with magnificent view of the Taj Mahal. Great photographs of the splendid monument can be taken from the garden. The Garden of Mehtab Bagh is a must visit from the tourists visiting the place.

The Tomb of Itmad-Ud-Daulah

The tomb signifies the usage of Red Sandstone in Mughal architecture, but initially the tomb was to be built with white marble. The tomb is known as an early draft for the Taj Mahal. It is said, various architectural techniques used in the Itmad-Ud-Daulah tomb have been used in the Taj. Various peaceful and beautiful gardens surround the Itmad-Ud-Daulah signify a rich and decorous taste.

The Kinari Bazar

The Kinari bazaar provides the tourists with a taste of ancient Agra. The narrow lanes and the colorful shops in the bazar can transport the tourists to the age of the "Badshahs"s and "Shehnshah"s. The voice of the shopkeepers bargaining, the small and beautifully decorated shops are an experience which will be repented if missed. The Kinari bazaar provides the tourists with unique clothing and shoes of Agra, the famous marble works of Agra, and not to be missed, the famous street snacks of the Bazaar. Various beautiful groom veils and turbans are also available in the Kinari Bazar. The bazaar generally opens at 11 30 am and closes at 6 30 pm.

The Fatehpur Sikri

The Fatehpur Sikri is an important stop in your Agra trip. The place lies at a distance of nearly 35Km from the main city of Agra. The Fatehpur Sikri was built by emperor Akbar and contains various places such as the Diwan-e-Khas and the Diwan-e-Aam. The famous Buland Darwaja is a symbol of magnificence and power. The house of Birbal, the Panchmahal, are must visits of Fatehpur Sikri.

Jaswant Singhs Chhattri

The date of construction of the Chhattri of Raja Jaswant Singh goes back to the years of 1654-58. The chhattri happens to be the only Hindu building in the Mughal regime. The beautiful chhattri is dedicated to Rani Hada. The Shekhawati architecture of Rajasthan has been represented in the chhattri. There happens to b a resemblance between the structure of the Agra Fort and the chhattri.

Sikandra

Sikandra happens to be one of the exponential symbols of the blend of Hindu and Muslim architecture. The resting place of Emperor Akbar is situated at a distance of 16 kms from Taj Mahal and happens to be one of the most popular monuments, attracting large number of tourists. The construction of Sikandra began in the year 1613 by Jahangir, the son of Emperor Akbar.

Chapter 6: Best Restaurants in Agra

Picture Courtesy: TripAdvisor

Agra's people love eating. Irrespective of whether it is a party or a business gathering, the spread on the table is amazing. Agra cuisine comprises all types of dishes. They are mainly regional. This is because people from different states reside in the city. As such the restaurants serve different types of cuisine.

We take a look at ten of the best restaurants for local food and other Indian cuisines in Agra:

Esphahan

Esphahan happens to be one of the finest restaurants in Agra. If you are planning to visit the restaurant, you need to make reservations in advance. The Esphahan is located inside the Oberoi Amarvillas Hotel, and provides its guests with one of the finest cuisines of North India. Guests usually have dinner listening to the live santoor players.

Shankar Ji

The Shankar Ji happens to be a local dhaba which lies close to a rickshaw stand. The dhaba offers one of the best local dishes of Agra. The atmosphere of the dhaba is pleasant, cozy and traditional, with lots of smiling faces to greet the tourists. A tourist may taste the best of local Indian dishes at Shankar Ji.

The Pinch of Spice

The restaurant Pinch of Spice is not located within a hotel, and serves the best of North Indian chicken tikka and chicken kebabs. A tourist will experience the best of the Indian spices. The Pinch of Spice is located in the Fatehabad Road, having a huge space for guest accommodation. Guests can have a wonderful view of the Taj while having their food.

Joneys Place

The Joneys Place is immensely famous among the tourists as the restaurant has a superb atmosphere with great food at affordable prices. The banana lassi and the 'malai kofta' served by the restaurant are essentially not to be missed. The restaurant has been preparing great lassi since 1978.

ShankaraVegis

The famous ShankaraVegis lies on the way to the Taj, offering one of the best quality Indian thalis at affordable prices. The beautiful rooftop view of the restaurant is not to be missed. The informal atmosphere of the restaurant plays a big role in attracting tourists. The restaurant is a must visit.

Jahanpana

The Jahanpana is experimentative, exploring the various undiscovered tastes of India. Awadhi cuisines happens to be there speciality. The various dishes such as gawlat kebabs and biriyani are great and prepared by highly trained cooks. The dum style in cooking are keenly taught to the apprentice chefs of this restaurant by the head chef.

The Lakshmi Villas

The Lakshmi Villas serves its guests with the best quality South Indian dishes. Various South Indian thalis happen to be its specialty. The down to earth approach of the restaurant and its superb food has made it immensely famous in Agra.

The Jhankar Retaurant

The Jhankar Retaurant is immensely popular, serving its guests with various mouth-watering dishes. The restaurant is open nightlong, with live music and dance. Guests enjoy traditional Indian dishes along with other cuisines. Magazi Murgh Korma and Dried Potato with coriander sauce happens to be the main attractions of this restaurant.

The Stuff Maker

The restaurant is located on the roof of Hotel Komal, and provides a magnificent view of the famous Taj Mahal to its guests. The restaurant serves its guests with the best of Agra's delicacies along with a mixture of global delicacies such as pancakes. The restaurant provides its guests with lunch, dinner, and breakfast.

Conclusion

It was the Mughals who introduced tandoor in the country. Tandoor is basically an earthen oven. Kababs are quite common in this part of the country. Kababs are small pieces of meat or chicken marinated in different spices. Thereafter, it is cooked over a coal tandoor. Many of the most prestigious and highly-regarded restaurants in Agra do not, in fact, serve Indian food, with awards lists dominated by Japanese, Italian, French and Chinese restaurants. There remains, however, a thriving scene for Indian food.

Chapter 7: Most Luxurious Hotels in Agra

Picture Courtesy: Booking.com

The Oberoi Amarvilas

The hotel lies at a distance of nearly 600 meters from the magnificent Taj. Its a luxury hotel providing tourists with each and every luxury amenity. The hotel comprises of nearly four dining accommodations and happens to be one of the most celebrated five star hotels in Agra. The basic characteristics of the Hotel Oberoi Amarvilas are free parking space for the tourists and free wi fi.

The Trident Agra

The Trident Agra is located at a distance of nearly 1.5 Km from the Taj Mahal. The basic amenities provided by the hotel include an outdoor pool, and a 24 hour help desk. The hotel consists of a bar, which is magnificent, and tourists can opt for rooms which are pool facing. The hotel provides the tourists with free wi fi. The hotel also comprises of a business center.

ITC Mughal a Luxury Collection Hotel

The ITC Mughal happens to be another most celebrated 5 stars hotels in Agra. The dining arrangement of the hotel serves its guests with Peshawari serving North West Frontier delights and Taj Bano. The hotel comprises of a three meal buffet, serving its guests with various traditional Indian specialties. Maikhana happens to be a lounge bar in the hotel, providing the tourists with a magnificent view of the garden, serving refreshing beverages to the tourists. You can essentially opt for the hotel if you are planning to visit Agra. The royal atmosphere of the hotel will be pampering you to the fullest.

The Radisson Blue Agra

Hotel Radisson Blue Agra is situated in the eastern gate of the Taj Mahal. The Hotel offers tourists with all the luxurious amenities possible. The hotel provides its tourists with a health club and a spa. The health club consists of an infinity pool. The hotel also offers its tourists with 5 dining options, from which the tourist can select. The hotel carries a good review along with itself, therefore it is essentially preferable.

The Gateway Hotel in Fatehabad

The Gateway Hotel in Fatehabad Agra, is situated on an area of nearly 9 acres and provides its tourists with immense luxury. The hotel provides its tourists with a magnificent view of The Taj Mahal.

Crystal Sarovar Premiere

Hotel Crystal Sarovar Premiere is located at a distance of nearly 1.2 kilometers from the Taj Mahal. The hotel is situated in the Taj Ganj area. Basic facilities offered by the hotel include free wi fi. The decorous arrangement of the hotel will be attracting you, therefore opt for the hotel.

The Ramada Plaza

Hotel Ramada Plaza in Agra happens to be one of the most luxurious hotels. A swimming pool which is outdoor and open throughout the year and a magnificent garden are the main attractions of the hotel. Enjoy living life king size with a magnificent game room, and free private parking.

Hotel Clarks Shiraz

The Hotel Clarks Shiraz is situated at a distance of nearly 0.9 mi from the Taj Mahal and the Ara Fort. The hotels offers its tourists with an outdoor swimming pool, a spa, and a wellness center. You can always opt for the Clarks Shiraz in case you want absolute luxury.

Double Tree Agra

The Double Tree Hotel located in Agra, serves its tourists with the prime facilities of luxury such as an outdoor swimming pool, a spa, and a wellness center. The Hotel also serves its tourists with wi fi in the proper areas of the hotel. The hotel carries tremendous goodwill along with it, and you need not hesitate before booking it.

Jaypee Palace Agra

The Jaypee Palace Agra is situated at a distance of nearly 1.6 mi from the Taj mahal. The hotel features magnificent water bodies to its tourists. Various landscaped gardens and ponds featured by the hotel happen to be its primary attractions.

Chapter 8: Things to Avoid in Agra

Picture Courtesy: Yatra Blog

Agra is one of the most lively, diverse, and strangely wonderful cities in which you can choose to stay. But in the face of an entirely different culture, it can also seem chaotic and intimidating to the first time visitor. Fear not, however – acclimating is half the fun. Eventually you will come to feel oddly at home walking down those bustling streets, but in the meantime here are some quick survival tips to help you adjust. If by the end of this list you are not scared off, then the adventure of a lifetime may be just around the corner.

Don't ever trust a stranger

Remember the times when your parents asked you to stay away from strangers? We may have ignored that warning over time, but don't make that mistake here in Agra. Chances are that you might be interacting with a professional crook or someone from a small town trying to make a fast buck. There are all sorts of people in the city— beware of whom you interact with!

- Take a break- On that same note, just give yourself a break some days and enjoy the little things in the city.

Don't skip Big Chill

Yes! Agra has a number of restaurants all over, but if you plan to give Big Chill a miss, your trip will remain incomplete.

- Some say it is overrated and overpriced, but we know that their desserts are absolutely worth dying for.

Beware of your belly

Like we mentioned before, Agra will tempt you into trying out the delicious street food. But while you indulge your taste buds, make sure not to overdo it or eat at the wrong places.

- Be wary of where you eat or drink from—no matter how hungry or thirsty you are.

Avoid Monsoon season

The best months to visit Agra are November–March, especially for people who can't bear the scorching sun, humidity or the water-logged roads of Agra monsoon. Agra winters are both pleasant and amazing, particularly in the mornings. Enjoy the morning breeze of Agra winters.

- Not every bathroom in India is equipped with toilet paper, so it's a good idea to carry some while travelling. Even though the condition of public bathrooms has improved, the ones in restaurants tend to be better options.

Drink bottled water

The tap water in Agra is not fit to drink from the source, so – unless you are a guest of someone who has a water purifier – make it a rule to only drink bottled water and avoid ice in drinks at bars and restaurants. This will reduce your chances of feeling unwell and not enjoying your trip.

- Never take drinks from strangers, and don't leave drinks unattended. Stay away from open street food.

Chapter 9: Best weekend Destinations of Agra

Picture Courtesy: Culture Trip

New Delhi

The capital city of India, New Delhi is situated near the city of Agra. The magnificent wonders of the city having immense historical significance are sure to attract you. The various places such as Cannaught Place, DilliHaat, Lajpat Nagar, etc are the prime shopping destinations of the city. Don't miss out Chandni Chowk. The city of Delhi has perhaps the best street side food in India, therefore taste the best of Delhi but be careful of your belly. You can also visit the various historical destinations in Delhi such as the Red Fort, Humayuns Tomb, etc.

- Delhi is the political and cultural capital of India.

Gwalior

Gwalior, the place of Miyan Tansen. The city of Gwalior is associated with various historical significances. The Gwalior Gharana in Indian Calssical music holds an exponential position. The city of Gwallior is immensely famous for its magnificent hilltop fort. The Tigra Dam, which is located at a distance of nearly 23 km from the city is a magnificent place to relax, therefore opt for Gwallior as a weekend destination.

Mathura

The city of Mathura hosts the biggest holi celebrations in the country during spring. Various magnificent paintings are associated to the city of Mathura, and a lover of art will love to roam around the city. The city of Mathura is immensely significant, as mythically, the birth of Lord Krishna is associated to the city. The city is always playful, with various places to explore and various items to buy. The city of Brindavan, at a distance of nearly 12 km from the city of Mathura, is immensely famous for its various temples.

- This place is one of the most holy cities of India.

- The Vrindavan city near Mathura is also of great prominence

Sultanpur Bird Sanctuary

This is a very beautiful place situated near Agra. This happens to be a perfect place for the bird loving person, where they can see many species of birds here. This place is engraved within a lush green mountain area. Some of the birds here are little cormorant, gray francolin, Indian roller, purple sunbird, black headed ibis, Siberian cranes, common teal, common teal, etc. These birds look very attractive. This is a really wonderful place for tourists.

- There are many migratory birds coming here from Siberia and other parts of Europe

- The area around Sultanpur is known as "Dhundhoti".

Bharatpur

This is wonderful place located near Agra. This place has some of the beautiful sceneries, which lures many of the people of Agra . This place is located at a height of 600 ft. The prime attraction of the people coming here is the Keoladeo National Park. This park is rich in floral and faunal diversity. This place definitely comes out as a very nice place for the visiting tourists.

- Bharatpur is also known as "Lohagarh" and the "Eastern Gateway to Rajasthan"

The Keoladeo National Park is included in the World Heritage Site list.

Haridwar

This is a very sacred place for Hindus located near Agra. The people of Agra visit this holy place whenever possible to have gain some peace of mind. The famous Kumbh Mela is also held in Haridwar pulling lakhs of the people here. There are many temples here too. This place definitely makes people joyous.

- This is one of the seven holiest (SaptaPuri) places for Hindus in the world

- The sacred Brahma Kund is also found in this place.

Mussoorie

This is a very popular tourist destination in India, which is located around 290 km from the Agra. This place appears almost like a 'fairyland' for the travelers coming here. The place is nicely located in the lush green valleys of the Shiwalik ranges, making many of the tourists delirious with its beautiful scenery. This is a perfect place for the trek loving tourist. Many people from Agra visit here for holidays.

- This place is also called "Gateway" to Gangotri and Yamunotri

- Nahata Estate, Kempty Falls, Mussoorie Lake, Bhatta Falls are some of the most visited places here.

Chapter 10: Conclusion

As we have mentioned earlier, Agra is a city which is historically immensely significant. Each lane and bylane of the city have a tale to narrate its visitors. The colourful atmosphere of the city has attracted tourists from a worldwide range, therefore, if you are planning to visit India, keep Agra under your category of "must visits".

Delhi

Essential Travel Tips – all you NEED to know

Copyright 2018 by Sam's Travel Guide - All rights reserved.

The contents of this book may not be reproduced, duplicated or transmitted without direct permission from the author.

Table of Contents

Chapter 1: Introduction..85

Chapter 2: Things You Must Know About Delhi..........88

Chapter 3: Best Places to Visit in Delhi............................91

Chapter 4: Best Travel Tips for Delhi................................99

Chapter 5: Famous Architectural Wonders in Delhi 105

Chapter 6: Best Restaurants in Delhi............................ 109

Chapter 7: Most Luxurious Hotels in Delhi.................115

Chapter 8: Weekend destinations in Delhi.................117

Chapter 9: Things to Avoid in Delhi............................123

Chapter 10: Conclusion...129

Chapter 1: Introduction

Picture Courtesy: Internshala blog

Delhi, the capital of India.

A historical city with an eclectic mix of tradition and modernity. The city of Delhi has been immensely significant, both historically and politically. Delhi has been the capital of India since the British period, having Kolkata as its predecessor. Reminicenses of "Indraprastha", which happened to be the capital of the Pandavas, and the information about which is be available in the great epic of The Mahabharata, are sill available in the city of Delhi, which depicts its existance right from the ancient ages. Owing to the discovery of an ancient inscription of the great Mauryan Emporer Ashoka near Srinivaspuri, we can conclude the ancient History of Delhi to be glorius and significant. Delhi has been a happening city with various incidents, be it political or cultural, taking place on a constant basis. In the year 1192, King Prithviraj Chauhan was defeated by an Afghan conqueror named Muhammad Ghori, and around 1200 AD came the death of native Hindu reistance, having foreign Turk and Muslim rulers as the principal emperors of the city for the next five centuries. Delhi has been significant in terms of witnessing various political incidents during the British period, along with the massive Hindu and Muslim riots, and the flag hoistage after the independence of India from the Lal Quilla, along with a magnificent performance by Ustaad Bismillah han. Delhi received its name "New Delhi" in the year 1927.

The city of Delhi is bordered by Haryana on its three sides, having Uttar Pradesh on its East. Not only did the city serve as the capital of India during the British period, but various kings and emporers had the city as their capital, principally because of its cosmopolitan approach and centralized position. Delhi presently happens to be the cultural and political capital of India, containing the various cultural and political institution's headquarters of the country in its belly. The city consists of the Indian Parliament, the National School of Drama, which happens to be the headquarters of theatre in India, and the Lalit Kala Kendra. Old Delhi consists of the lanes and bylanes of Chandni Chawk which have various stories to narrate to its visitors. Chandni Chowk happens to be the carnival point of Delhi, since the advent of the foreign rulers. Delhi, also happens to be the hub of education with prestigious universities such as the JNU(Jawaharlal Universiy) and the DU(Delhi University).

Chapter 2: Things You Must Know About Delhi

Picture Courtesy: The Independent

Population

Delhi happens to be the second most populated city in the world after Tokyo. Delhi, being the capital of India has been highly populated right from the time of the foreign rulers. The centralized location of the city makes it an ideal place to live in, with the essential requirements right at hand. This is the main factor which has played a role in converting Delhi into the second most populated city of the world. Presently the city of Delhi consists of approximately 25 million inhabitants. As per the census report of 2015, the city consisted of approximately 18.2 million inhabitants back then.

Spices of Delhi

The Khari Baoli market in Delhi happens to be the largest spice hub in Asia. The Khari Baoli market has been immensely significant within the city since the seventeenth century, and various items such as nuts, herbs and all kinds of spices are sold in the place. The Khari Baoli market located near the Red Fort and the western end of the Chandni Chowk, happens to be a wholesale market for spices. You must visit the Khari Baoli market in order to feel the flavours of Old Delhi, and experience the carnivalistic feel of the city.

The Capital City

Calcutta or Kolkata happened to be the capital of India upto 1911. The Parition of Bengal, a decision which was taken by the then Viceroy Lord Curzon, led to great political unrest in the city. Protests and agitations, along with the murder of various government officials in the city contitued to happen. Such a botched up situation led to the transfer of the capital from Kolkata to Delhi. Since then, Delhi continued to be the capital of India.

Delhi, the city of Gates

Delhi happens to be famous for its gates which have tremendous historical significance. The gates of the city have antidiluvian stories to narrate to its visitors. Five of the most significant gates of the city are, Kashmiri gate, Lahori Gate, Delhi Gate, Ajmeri Gate and Turkman Gate. If you are planning to visit Delhi, then take a look at the gates of the city. The past, along with a tinge of the present ihois going to haunt you and extract your appreciation.

Delhi, the biggest city within India

Earlier we have known Delhi to be the most populated city in India, but now we also come to know about the fact of Delhi being the biggest city in India area wise. 1942 sq km happens to be the size of the city, which is vast. The city of Delhi is even biger than the cities of Bengaluru or Mumbai. Not only in terms of size, New Delhi also happens to be the second most wealthy cities in India after Mumbai.

Chapter 3: Best Places to Visit in Delhi

Picture Courtesy: Treebo

Chandni Chowk

Chandni Chowk is sort of like Delhi's Times Square. This narrow street of Delhi is best visited on foot as there is scarcity for space. The street is busy at any time of the day with customers, vendors, rickshaws, and locals moving through it. Chandni Chowk is one stretch that has stores and markets that offer good quality products at shockingly low prices. The market of Chandni Chowk is very old. The origin of Chandni Chowk dates back to the Mughal era in Indian history. According to legend, Chandni Chowk market was established during the reign of the Mughal Emperor Shahjahan. The legend also says that Chandni Chowk market was designed by Jahanara-Emperor Shahjahan's favorite daughter. A large 'chowk' or square with a centrally located pool was incorporated in the initial design. Chandni chowk is always buzzing with life. The environment here is electric. Waves of people can sweep you away if you remain standing for a moment on the street. It doesn't take a scientist to know that it is one of the busiest hubs in the entire country and in the world too. It can aptly be called a living museum.

Red Fort

The monument that Delhi is most famous for is the Red Fort. The fort was built when the Mughal Empire ruled over India, around the 16th century. The fort has an Indian flag that is hoisted on August 15 each year marking India's independence. The fort stretches for around 1.2 miles (1.9 kms) and has been standing strong ever since. The Red Fort was constructed with red sandstone which happens to be the main reason for its name being Red Fort. Presently the monument has been turned into a museum, which presents the various articles used in the past. The Red Fort served as the main residence of the Mughal Emperors for nearly 200 hundred years, and its political significance as a monument has attracted tourists from across the world. The various precious art works and jewels within the Red Fort were plundered by both Nadir Shah and the British. If you are planning to visit Delhi, do not miss the famous Moti Masjid or the Pearl Mosque. The Moti Masjid which is situated within the Red Fort is not only beautiful but at the same time historically significant. The beautiful Moti Masjid was built by Emperor Aurangzeb. Experience the magnificence of the glorious Red Fort, which certainly demands a visit.

Humayun's Tomb

Humayun's Tomb was built for Humayun's burial in the 15th century. The architecture of the Tomb is surreal and fits the definition of the word scenic in every way. It also inspired the design of a wonderful marvel of the world, the Taj Mahal in Agra. It was the first of many monuments built for Mughal emperors. The construction of Humayun's Tomb has been chiefly inspired by Persian and other Central Asian architectures which have played a role in creating its immense beauty. The Humayun's Tomb is surrounded by beautiful gardens, which is a must watch if you are planning to go to the place. Other buildings which are associated to the complex of the Humayun's Tomb also demand a visit from you as a tourist. You can opt for guides who are available within the premises of the Tombs, but remember to be careful of frauds. Various Guide Books are available for sale which can guide you around the interiors of the Tomb. The Humayun's Tomb is located on a centralized position; therefore you will not be facing many difficulties to visit the place.

Jama Masjid

The Jama Masjid is a treat of the old city. It has been one of the many famous monuments that have been etched in history. It is the largest mosque in India with a capacity of seating over 25000 devotees. The mosque's towers offer a beautiful view of the city of Delhi. The Jama Masjid is situated in a walking distance from Old Delhi Railway station and ISBT Kashmere

Gate. Chawri Bazaar is the nearest Metro Station – some 500m away. AC and non-AC buses connect Jama Masjid to the entire city of Delhi. Autos and taxis can also be availed to reach here. The Jama Masjid is open from 7am to 12pm, 1:30pm to 6:30pm, all days of the week, the entry fee is Rs 200-300. An extra amount of Rs 100 is charged for photography. The beautiful Jama Masjid was built by Emperor Shah Jahan. The huge minarets of the Jama Masjid were constructed by using red sand stone and white marble, which make it so beautiful. The Jama Masjid remained as the royal mosque of the Mughal emperors, till the advent of the later conquerors. If you are visiting Delhi, then you must perceive the royal essence of the Jama Masjid, the atmosphere of which is not only royal in nature but also a place for benediction.

The Qutub Minar

Another prime example of Mughal architecture in Delhi is the Qutub Minar. The minar currently stands as the tallest brick minaret in the world. As an example of durability the minar has been standing for over 800 years. With an unclear historical background, the minar is said to signify the beginning of Mughal rule in India. Earlier tourists were allowed to climb to the top of the minar, but presently you will have to enjoy it only by observing it from the outside. The Qutub Minar has its history of being constructed by three consecutive emperors, Qutub-ud-din Aibak, the founder of the Delhi Sultanate, who started the construction, Iltutmish, who added to the construction, and finally Sher Shah Suri, who finished the construction. The famous iron pillar of Delhi is adjacent to the Minar. Strange stories associated to the pillar of Delhi attract tourists in large numbers. Stories of wish fulfillment associated to the pillar of Delhi instigate immense interest amongst the visitors. The Qutub Minar also contains the famous Quat-Ul Islam Mosque within it, which must be visited by you. Although various incidents of earthquakes and other natural calamities have been causing serious damage to the Qutub Minar, still the minar stands strong, attracting a huge number of tourists annually.

The India Gate

When you think of Delhi, India Gate, the war memorial monument comes to mind. The significance of the place, as a way to pay respect to the people who sacrificed their lives for the safety of the nation, is tremendous. It is one of the most popular destinations of tourist attraction. The India Gate was constructed in order to pay tribute to the 70,000 soldiers belonging to the British India who died during the period of First World War. Sir Edwin Lutyens was the designer of India Gate. The design of India Gate has received its inspiration from Roman architecture, and is appreciated throughout the world. The parade of Republic Day begins from Rashtrapati Bhavan and passes through India Gate, which signifies valor and martyrdom. If you are planning to visit Delhi, then you must necessarily pay a visit to the India Gate in order to appreciate its essence. The monument has further been used in various movies and stories.

The Bahai Temple

One of the finest evidences of brilliant architecture is the Bahai Temple. Popularly known as the Lotus temple, the temple building is shaped, you guessed it right, in the form of a lotus. Made entirely out of White marble, the temple is just as attractive on the inside as it is on the outside. As per the reports of various popular news channels, The Bahai Temple happens to be one of the most visited buildings in the world. The approach of the Bahai Temple is secular, and it is open to people of every religious belief, wherefore, you need not be a Bahai in order to appreciate the beauty of the Bahai Temple. The Bahai Temple has gained its inspiration from the lotus, which has further played a role in its construction. Nine doorways lead to a central hall of the temple, and such a unique construction gains appreciation and attraction worldwide. If you are visiting Delhi, then you must visit the Bahai Temple, without which you may have the possibilities of repenting your trip.

The Gandhi Smriti or the Raj Ghat

It was on January 30, 1948 that Mohandas Karamchand Gandhi was assassinated. He is also referred to as the father of the nation for driving India to peace using non-violence. The Gandhi Smriti is the spot where he was shot and collapsed. The place was turned into a prayer house open to the public to pay their respects to the peacemaker. Mohandas Karamchand Gandhi, the father of the nation, dwells within the memories of people. The Raj Ghat, or Gandhi Smriti, is frequently visited by politicians from all over the world. A flame burning in Raj Ghat is eternal which depicts the eternal spirit of the great martyr and the father of our nation. If you are visiting the Gandhi Smriti or Raj Ghat, which you must, you will not face much difficulty, as the place stands in a central location.

The Lodi Gardens

If you're looking for a relaxed day away from work and the stress of a fast-paced city life, Lodi Gardens is the place to be. It is one destination to enjoy nature at its finest with the gardens offering a tranquil ambience. On a regular day, you'll find people jogging, exercising, practicing yoga together, and a few young couples that are here to spend time together. The Lodi Gardens happen to be a creation of 15th century by the Lodis, and the place is spread over a huge area of nearly 90 acres. The situation of the Lodi Gardens in between Safdarjung Tomb and Khan Market and it is very popular, as a good number of tourists and morning walkers visit the area every day. The Lodi Gardens is popular among the dwellers of Delhi, and every morning, lots of people gather around the area to perform their morning fitness regimen. Enjoy some fresh air from this historical relic, which will grant you immense peace and satisfaction.

The Swaminarayan Akhshardham Temple

A fairly new symbol of modern architecture is the temple of Swaminarayan Akshardham. Conceptually designed to offer prayers, the temple completed construction and was open to the public in 2005. The pink stone and white marble stone used signify its importance. The magnificent architecture of the Swaminarayan Akshardham Temple has achieved immense success in creating an aura among the tourists. The temple of the Swaminarayan Akshardham was officially inaugurated by the former president of India, Mr. APJ Abdul Kalam and the temple maintains a strict vastushastra. If you are planning to visit Delhi then you must pay a visit to the Swaminarayan Akshardham temple which guaranties benediction. Various precious articles such as the Rajasthan pink sandstone and the Italian Carrara Marble have been used in order to create this magnificent temple. The various exhibits of the temple create immense aura within the tourists. India being a land of Mystic culture provides her tourists with such magnificent attractions, which, if you miss, will lead to a great repentance.

Chapter 4: Best Travel Tips for Delhi

Picture Courtesy: Ginger Hotels

The capital of the country of India, Delhi is a busy city that is proud of its fast-paced lifestyle, rich history, cultural diversity, and its technological advancements. An authentic Delhi experience offers a volume that might be hard to absorb for a first-time visitor. This post offers ten travel tips for Delhi that might make your journey a happy one.

Street beggars of Delhi

Beggars are a common sight on the streets of India. While it's noble to offer money, it's best that you don't entertain them. Even though you may stick to an emotional premise and offer, it is important to stay practical, keep your money to yourself and avoid promoting lethargy unknowingly. Plus, you'll also be attracting the other beggars close by as you offer one. Poverty happens to be a principal problem in the country of India, which gives rise to the pathetic situation of beggary. Beggary happens to be an age old practice in the country of India and there is nothing new or sudden in it. Beggars usually choose religious places in order to ask money in return of nothing, no reciprocation. Although the sight is pathetic, but trying to be a messiah can be problematic, as many of them can catch you up and ask for money. So be aware and deal the situation tactfully.

Explore and Escape

With so much to explore in the city, you should maintain a balance between exploration and escape. A key component of a happy journey to India is taking adequate rest. Before going about the city to experience a new place, you can rest by reading books, listening to music, or watch a Bollywood movie. Delhi being an extremely historical city, you have a lot to explore around. Do not rush up, or else you may end up in a botched up situation. Taste the best tastes of the famous restaurants in Connaught Place, taste the delicious ice creams of Nirula's and last but not the least, do get a bite of the famous Sohan Halwa, the local taste of Delhi, which will not be failing to create an awe!

Exchange your currency

If you are a tourist carrying foreign currency with you, then you need not worry. There are options for exchanging your currency. Whenever you are in a foreign country, be it in India or elsewhere, one of the most important issues is to get hold of the local currency. Finding the local currency exchange is always a tough business, as there are often cheats around, and in some cases, you may end up with the worst exchange rates possible. Independent money lending shops, or shops which are associated to the forex chains are the best in terms of exchanging money. A commercial area such as Connaught Place or Paharganj, are the best place which may help you out in case you fall in any trouble related to currency.

Keep yourself clean

Delhi isn't a clean city known for its maintenance. More often than not, you'll find waste dumped into random public places, water leakage, and dirty water bodies. In an environment like this, it is important to keep yourself clean, drink packaged drinking water, and use a sanitizer. Various construction works in the city of Delhi have generated a huge amount of waste products and dust leading to thick smog, wherefore, do not forget to keep yourself out of dust and always take the necessary precautions. Carry a mask along with yourself if necessary. It's good to remain associated with the locals of a place that has such a historical and cultural aura as Delhi has, but keep yourself out of the local hazards, which may ruin your health.

Be careful with your stomach

When in Delhi, It is important to follow your stomach, quite literally. Delhi's cuisine, though diverse with lip-smacking foods, requires acclimatization. The food is packed with flavors of the different spices of India and even troubles the locals at times. As a tourist, it is recommended that you experiment with your food choices very less. Once you are accustomed, you can have the rich food of Delhi but if it fails to suit you, you can have serious stomach issues, though they are quite avoidable in the first place if you are careful, so it is best to avoid oily and spicy food as much as possible.

Bargain your way out

Typically, I would never stress about bargaining as most cities in India don't cheat their foreign customers much. Delhi is an exception to that. Be it a local or an international tourist, the vendors are looking to exploit the customer to gain some extra profit. Bargain, if possible, to the half of the quoted price. Bargaining is an art, and once you adopt the techniques carefully, you become the winner. Delhi is a city selling various rare historical souvenirs, which do not have a fixed price attached to themselves; therefore don't give up until and unless you achieve success in buying your product. Various procedures to save money are to be keenly studied while travelling to Delhi.

Local souvenirs of Delhi

Delhi and its neighboring places are rich in handicrafts. Do not miss it even if you are short in time. But as usual, be careful to buy the right thing at the right price. Know the local markets well and if possible, take help from a trusted local. Delhi happens to be one of the most historical cities in India; therefore it is essential to buy souvenirs or to be more specific local souvenirs in Delhi. If you are planning to receive the best tastes of Delhi, then do not forget to collect its best souvenirs.

The various Madhubani paintings, magnificent Assamese silks, and varieties of pickles are the prime souvenirs, which you essentially need to collect. Last but not the least, do not forget the bargain policy, as most the times such items are sold in the open market.

The famous Delhi Rickshaw ride

Rickshaws are the fastest and most efficient modes of transportation in Delhi. Even though you may find a cab ride comforting and offering every bit of luxury, traffic in Delhi is one thing you can't get past. Unless you take a rickshaw, you'll find yourself running late almost always. Rickshaw rides offer a 'once-in-a-lifetime' experience that are fun and in a few cases, wild! Rickshaws happen to be an old and local tradition of Delhi, the efficient "rickshaw-walas" in Delhi provide the tourists and passengers with an all day long fun and frolic experience, therefore you need to make the most of the rickshaw rides in Delhi.

Go with the flow

In the list of busiest states, Delhi features at a high position with people keeping to their business unless the situation demands otherwise. Usually this affects the tourism experience. However, it is very important to go with the flow and not get bogged down. Keep your travel plans open and flexible, to enjoy the most. Delhi at times can be both fast as well as slow; you need to cope up with the speed in order to be associated with the immense fun and frolic of the city. If you fail to associate yourself with the speed of the city then you will be lagging behind, deprived of the fun and frolic of the city. Enjoy Delhi to its local levels, which provide you with its traditional tastes.

Clothes you should wear in Delhi

Delhi being an urban city, has benefited from the suit-and-tie MNC culture, and does not have any particular traditional dress outfit of its own. Most of the people living in Delhi wear casual comfort clothes. You'll also find people wearing professional formal clothes for work. However, to avoid any unpleasant experiences, it is always recommended you avoid obscenity. Decent clothes are recommended in the streets of Delhi. If you happen to be a foreigner, then you can try out the local outfits, going with the local traditions of India. Keep yourself comfortable. If you are planning to visit the city during summer time, remember to keep yourself cool, wear something casual, with light colors. Don't worry much about the outfits; Delhi accepts all types of vibrant colors.

Chapter 5: Famous Architectural Wonders in Delhi

Picture Courtesy: Rajasthan On Wheel Tours

We have stated some of the famous wonders of Delhi previously. Delhi happens to be a city of art and architecture, attracting tourists with its magnificent archeological reminiscences, which are a must visit.

The Jantar Mantar

The Jantar Mantar happens to be one of the most famous and ancient observatories in India. It is situated at a prime location of the city, which grants easy access to tourists. The Jantar Mantar was built by Msssaharaja Jaisingh of Udaipur, in the year 1794. Presently the Jantar Mantar attracts a huge number of tourists. The Jantar Mantar was built in order to observe the celestial bodies. The principal purpose of building the Jantar Mantar was deciding astronomical tables, observing the movements of celestial bodies such as the sun, the moon and the planets. The construction of Jantar Mantar is completely scientific, depicting the advancements in Indian science and technology. The Jantar Mantar colored in red, is situated near Connaught place, which is the principal reason for it being centralized with its position. If you are planning to tour around Delhi, the Jantar Mantar is a must see. This magnificent observatory with a rich historical background is sure to provide you with a taste of early India.

The Rashtrapati Bhavan

Rashtrapati Bhavan, the house of the President of India, is situated in the most centralized and significant location in Delhi. Entrance into the Rashtrapati Bhavan does not require any kind of entry fee. The Rashtrapati Bhavan attracts a huge number of tourists on a per day basis, who come to witness the magnificent building. The Rashtrapati Bhavan is opened from morning till night and the military parade on Republic Day begins from this famous building. Edwin Lutyens happens to be the designer of The Rashtrapati Bhavan, and the beautiful design still gives it a fresh and new approach. The royal approach of the building and the gardens associated to the building depict a decorous feel about the building. The gardens around the Rashtrapati Bhavan are open to the general public, which results in attracting more and more tourists. It's interesting to know that the construction of Rashtrapati Bhavan took 19 years. If you are planning to tour around Delhi, don't miss out this national pride of the country.

The Indian Parliament

The Parliament of India is one of the top political buildings of the country. The building is located in the most centralized position in New Delhi. It is the supreme legislative body of the Republic of India. The Parliament of India was designed by Edwin Lutyens and Herbert Baker. The construction of the Indian Parliament took six years to complete, and finally the building was inaugurated in the year 1927 by Lord Irwin. The Central Hall within the Indian Parliament contains the Lok Sabha, the Rajya Sabha and the Library Hall. The building is surrounded by gardens. Although a journey to the Indian Parliament might require special permission, but you must not miss a chance to grab the opportunity, which evinces extreme interest.

The Laxmi Narayan Temple

The Laxmi Narayan Temple was inaugurated by Mahatma Gandhi in the year 1939 and happens to be one of the most famous and significant temples in Delhi. This beautiful temple, which was built by the Birlas, pays tribute the Hindu God Vishnu, and the Hindu Goddess Laxmi. The place is frequented by a large number of tourists annually. The temple accepts visitors of all types of faith, which depicts India's true diversity. If you are searching for benediction and peace, then the Laxmi

Narayan Temple is just the right place for you, so do not lose a chance to pay a visit to the temple. The construction of temple depicts the true decorous approach of the country.

The Gurudwara Bangla Sahib

The Gurudwara Bangla Sahib earlier used to be a bunglow of Maharaja Jai Singh, and presently it happens to be one of the most popular gurudwaras in Delhi. The Grudwara Bangla Sahib is situated right in the heart of Connaught Place, and is frequented by lots of visitors. The Gurudwara Bangla Sahib is historically significant, and its history dates back right up to the time of Aurangzeb. Taking a dip in the holy waters of the Gurudwara Bangla Sahib is considered to be auspicious and lots of people come to take a dip in order to heal their sufferings. The Gurudwara has a legendary history of saving the residents of Delhi from a fierce epidemic. If peace and submission happen to be your demand, then Gurudwara Bangla Sahib happens to be your place. The construction of the Gurudwara depicts the traditional history of India.

Chapter 6: Best Restaurants in Delhi

Picture Courtesy: Vogue

Delhi-ites love eating. Irrespective of whether it is a party or a business gathering, the spread on the table is amazing. Delhi's cuisine comprises all types of dishes. They are regionally diverse as well. This is because people from different states reside in the capital city. As such the restaurants in Delhi serve different types of cuisine. Delhi was ruled by many dynasties. And every time the rulers settled here, they introduced different types of cuisine. Delhi was ruled by Afghans, English, Arabs, Rajputs, and Mughals etc.

We take a look at ten of the best restaurants for local food and other Indian cuisines in New Delhi:

Dum Pukht

Dum Pukht is an important feature of the Awadhi cuisine of Lucknow; meats, herbs and spices are placed in a pot that is then sealed with dough and slow-cooked over a very low flame. The meat cooks in its own juices, taking on the flavours of the seasoning, and resulting in a hearty and aromatic dish that is the specialty of this opulent restaurant that shares its name.

- Recently named the best restaurant in India in the S. Pellegrino and AcquaPanna list of Asia's fifty best restaurants, Dum Pukht serves its slow-cooked kebabs and biryanis in its extravagant blue-and-silver dining room, complete with crystal chandeliers.

Karim's

Serving the cuisine of the imperial kitchens of the Mughal Empire since 1913, Karim's is a very popular restaurant in New Delhi that has recently opened up at a number of new locations. Its hundred year old original premises besides the Jama Masjid in Old Delhi, however, remains the top destination for experiencing its renowned local dishes – mutton burra kebabs and the legendary tandoori chicken.

- A favorite with locals and tourists, the restaurant is a simple, no-frills and authentic dining experience.

Indian Accent

Housed in a small boutique hotel, Indian Accent is an innovative and unusual restaurant in New Delhi where chef Manish Mehrotra fuses local foods with contemporary international cuisine in new and unexpected ways, such as stuffing the North Indian specialty galawat lamb kebab with foie-gras and serving it with strawberry and green chilli chutney.

- Another favourite from the menu is soft-shell crab with roasted coconut and tomato pickle, while their butter chicken is altered with the addition of roast peanuts and peanut butter.

Moti Mahal

Moti Mahal in Daryaganj is one of Delhi's oldest surviving restaurants. Founded shortly after Indian independence in 1947, it claims to have introduced the recipes for tandoori chicken, butter chicken and burra kebabs to the local restaurant scene. It is a great place to sample these north Indian delicacies, and it has remained in its original premises with an internal courtyard and a simple, authentic atmosphere.

- Moti Mahal has expanded into a global chain with branches in almost every city in India.

Bukhara

Right next door to Dum Pukht in the ITC Maurya hotel, is another one of S. Pellegrino and AcquaPanna's 50 best Asian restaurants: the legendary Bukhara. In contrast to the extravagant Dum Pukht, Bukhara serves its internationally-renowned kebabs in a dining room of clay tiles and bare wood, and dishes appear without cutlery but with bibs.

- It opened in 1977 and has changed little since then; the menu still consists of marinated meats cooked in a tandoor, along with the famous black lentil and tomato dal, simmered for twenty four hours.

Panjabi By nature

Punjabi by Nature is another popular restaurant now expanding to multiple locations around Delhi. As the name suggests, it specializes in Punjabi cuisine, with particular favourites including Raan-e-Punjab (lamb's leg slow-roasted in a tandoor) and black lentils with butter and cream.

- Most famous of all are Punjabi by Nature's vodka golgappas: a twist on the popular street snack of puri, chutney, chickpeas, potatoes and onions, with the usual flavoured water in the filling replaced with spiced vodka.

Spice Route

Intricately designed to reflect the eastward journey of spices from the Malabar Coast in Kerala, through Sri Lanka, Burma and Thailand to Vietnam, Spice Route in the Imperial Hotel has a menu of pan-Asian cuisine. Standout options are Thai-style lobster stir fried with ginger and mushrooms, and vermicelli payasam with cashew nuts and raisins.

- The interiors are luxurious, with each of its rooms featuring hand painted murals and artefacts reflecting the many cultures along the route.

Dakshin

Dakshin, in the Sheraton New Delhi, serves a wide variety of foods from southern India, covering the states of Kerala, Andhra Pradesh, Tamil Nadu and Karnataka, and disposing of the Western view that all south Indian cuisine is vegetarians. Instead, Dakshin offers dishes including pan-fried sole, deep-fried prawns, and veinchinamamsam (lamb with onions, coriander, chillies and garam masala).

- The ingredients and spices for each dish are authentic and sourced from their home regions, and the southern Indian authenticity even extends to the art on the walls.

Varq

Another of the San Pellegrino and AcquaPanna's 50 best restaurants in Asia, Varq, at the Taj Hotel blends traditional Indian street food with modern expertise and experimentation, set in a sophisticated contemporary dining room.

- Chef Hemant Oberoi's new twists on old foods from the subcontinent include syrupy jalebi served with silver leaf and pistachio dip, ganderi chicken kebabs skewered on sugar cane, and attaraan: roast leg of lamb in a saffron dough shell.

Park Balluchi

Park Balluchi's Hauz Khas premises is located in the middle of Deer Park, affording diners stunning views and opportunities to observe the local wildlife from within the glass-walled restaurant. Park Balluchi's menu features a wide range of authentic Mughlai and Afghan barbecue dishes, such as murgpotli – minced lamb wrapped in marinated chicken breast – and grilled chicken marinated in saffron.

- For vegetarians, there is 'mewa paneer tukra': an elaborate dish of cottage cheese stuffed with nuts, dates and raisins.

Conclusion

It was the Mughals who introduced tandoor in the country. Tandoor is basically an earthen oven. Kababs are quite common in this part of the country. Kababs are small pieces of meat or chicken marinated in different spices. Thereafter, it is cooked over a coal tandoor. Many of the most prestigious and highly-regarded restaurants in New Delhi do not, in fact, serve Indian food, with awards lists dominated by Japanese, Italian, French and Chinese restaurants. There remains, however, a thriving scene for Indian food, and worldwide favourites such as tandoori chicken have their origins in the kitchens of New Delhi.

Chapter 7: Most Luxurious Hotels in Delhi

Picture Courtesy: Yatra.com

The Leela Palace New Delhi

The Hotel Leela Palace is located in New Delhi's Diplomatic Enclave, and holds a prestigious position among hotels in Delhi. The hotel is fully air conditioned and contains all the luxurious amenities.

The Lodhi

The Lodhi holds a proud position among the prestigious hotels of the world. The hotel is situated at a distance of 1km from Humanyun's Tomb, and contains an outdoor swimming pool along with other luxurious facilities.

The Imperial Hotel

The Imperial hotel in New Delhi is located at a distance of 1km from the City Center and Business district of Delhi. The hotel provides its customers with luxurious spas and other facilities. The hotel has been awarded the 2012 Trip Advisor Award For excellence.

The Pearl Premium Luxury Hotel

The Pearl Premium Luxury Hotel is situated at a distance of 5km from the Red Fort and provides its tourists with various facilities such as Free Wi fi.

The Holiday Inn at New Delhi Airport

The Holiday Inn at New Delhi is located within the International Airport of New Delhi, and offers its guest the best quality spa and other facilities. The hotel contains a luxurious swimming pool and offers free wifi.

Chapter 8: Weekend destinations in Delhi

Picture Courtesy: akshardham.com

Delhi is a very important city of India as it is the capital of this country. Delhi is quite a large metropolitan city, which is also important commercially. Compared to other big cities in India, Delhi has more pollution. People working here have hectic work schedules, and are constantly looking for places around Delhi which can make them stress free and they can have some enjoyable moments. There are many places around Delhi where people can visit in the weekends to rejuvenate themselves. Let us see some of the 10 popular weekend destinations around Delhi.

Hansi

Hansi is a beautiful place nearby Delhi which falls in the Haryana state. Hansi is located beautifully in a green mountainous region. This place also has some of the important archaeological monuments. The Asigarh fort is one of the important monuments located here. This fort belonged to the great Prithviraj Chauhan. This is an architecturally well-built fort. People from Delhi come here in large numbers to experience some peaceful moments.

- This fort is named as "Asigarh" because many of the swords were manufactured in this fort

- The Archaeological survey has declared this fort as a Protected Monument of National Importance.

Rishikesh

Rishikesh is a beautiful place located in Uttarakhand, which is about 230 kms(5 hrs drive) away from Delhi. This place is located at the foothills of the Himalayas. This place is religiously very important as many temples are found here. The swift flowing river here is another attraction for the tourists coming here. There are some of the best Yoga Ashrams here and people from all over the world come here to practice yoga.

- The Lakshman Jhula bridge is one of the main attractions for the people coming here

- This place is also known as "Gateway to the Garhwal Himalayas".

Mathura

Mathura is a very holy place located about 160 kilometers from Delhi. This place is religiously very important for Hindus, as Lord Krishna was born at this place. Any person coming to this place gets great religious satisfaction. Many people from Delhi visit this place and gain great peace of mind.

- This place is one of the holiest cities of India.
- The Vrindavan city near Mathura is also of great prominence

Kufri

Kufri is a very beautiful place in the North near Delhi. Compared to other places, this place is a bit far from Delhi. However, this place is really amazing as a large number of visitors come to this place. The trek loving people come here in big numbers as there are many awesome trekking routes. The zoological place located here is also visited by many people. This place is really amazing.

- Skiing is done in many of the places here.
- Kufri has more than 150 species of faunal diversity

Agra

Agra is a very well-known place in India and across the world as well. This place is about 210 kms from Delhi. The Taj Mahal is the most visited place by tourists visiting India. Apart from that, the Fatehpur Sikri and Agra Fort have also been attracting many of the tourists. The people of Delhi come here very often to enjoy the beautiful climate and have some moments along with these monuments. Agra is a one of the most visited places by people of Delhi.

- The UNESCO has included the Tāj Mahal, Agra Fort and Fatehpūr Sikrī in World Heritage Sites list, all of which are located in Agra

- Shauripur of Jainism and Runukta of Hinduism have links to Agra

Dehradun

Dehradun happens to be another amazing place near Delhi. Located about 245 kms from Delhi, this place has been successful in luring people from Delhi in weekends. Dehradun has many picturesque places which are simply mind blowing. People coming here can refresh their mind in these beautiful lush green valleys.

- Dehradun is situated between river Ganga and river Yamuna

- Dehradun is also known as one of the "Counter Magnets"

Sultanpur Bird Sanctuary

Sultanpur Bird Sanctuary is a very beautiful place which is situated just 40 km away from Delhi. This happens to be a perfect place for the average bird lover, as they can see many species of birds here. This place is surrounded by a lush green mountainous area. Some of the birds here are little cormorant, gray francolin, Indian roller, purple sunbird, black headed ibis, Siberian cranes, common teal etc. These birds look very attractive in their different hues in the backdrop of green vegetation. This is a really nice place for tourists.

- There are many migratory birds coming here from Siberia and other parts of Europe
- The nearby area around Sultanpur is known as "Dhundhoti".

Haridwar

Haridwar is a very sacred place for Hindus which is located about 210 kilometers from Delhi. People from Delhi visit this holy place whenever possible for attaining some peace of mind. The famous Kumbh Mela is also held in Haridwar attracting lakhs of devotees. There are many temples here too. This place definitely gives a lot of happiness to its visitors.

- This is one of the seven holiest (SaptaPuri) places for Hindus in the world
- The sacred Brahma Kund place is also found in this place

Bharatpur

Bharatpur is a very wonderful place located around 180 km from the Delhi. This place has some of the most beautiful sceneries, which lures many people from Delhi . This place is located at a height of 600 ft. The prime attraction of the people coming here is the Keoladeo National Park . This park is rich in floral and faunal diversity. This place definitely comes out as a very nice option for people looking for recreational spots in weekends.

- Bharatpur is also known as "Lohagarh" and the "Eastern Gateway to Rajasthan"

- The Keoladeo National Park is also a World Heritage Site.

Musoorie

Mussoorie is a very popular tourist destination in India, which is located around 290 km from Delhi. This place appears almost like a 'fairyland' for travelers coming here. The place is nicely located in the lush green valleys and Shiwalik ranges, making many of the tourists loose themselves in the peaceful surroundings. This is a perfect place for the trek loving tourist. Many people from Delhi visit here during holidays.

- This place is also called the "Gateway to Gangotri and Yamunotri"

- Nahata Estate, Kempty Falls, Mussoorie Lake, Bhatta Falls are some of the most visited place here.

Chapter 9: Things to Avoid in Delhi

Picture Courtesy: tripoto.com

New Delhi is one of the most lively, diverse, and strangely wonderful cities which you can choose to visit. But in the face of an entirely different culture, it can also seem chaotic and intimidating to the first time visitor. Fear not, however – acclimatizing is half the fun. Eventually you will come to feel oddly at home walking down those bustling streets, but in the meantime here are some quick survival tips to help you get by with ease. If by the end of this list you are not scared off, then the adventure of a lifetime may be just around the corner.

1. Don't ever trust a stranger
Remember the times when your parents asked you to stay away from strangers? We may have ignored the warning over time, but don't make that mistake here in Delhi. Chances are that you

might be interacting with a professional crook or someone from a small town trying to make a fast buck. There are all sorts of people in the capital city—be wary of whom you interact with!.

- Take a break- On that same note, just give yourself a break some days and enjoy the little things in the capital. Watch a movie at a cinema hall, check out the bookstores, enjoy a nice meal or go to a parlor for some pampering (many parlors and spas in Delhi offer packaged deals).

2. Don't get your hair beaded at DilliHaat

Yes, the idea of getting your hair beaded with various colors at DilliHaat might be appealing—but it is not worth it! The ladies at DilliHaat might promise how easy it would be to remove later, but it really isn't. Several tourists like to get it done and keep it on for a few days, but get hassled at the end of it all by the endless number hair knots. Not something you'd want to remember! Divide major areas and markets you want to visit and explore one of them in a day. Try to relax and enjoy every place you visit. Chances are, things won't go according to plan in this chaotic city, so adapt and go with the flow.

- Make a list of must-see places (a few suggestions are: Red Fort, Chandni Chowk, India Gate, Humayun's Tomb, Connaught Place, Khan Market) and enjoy the city, one day at a time.

3. Don't skip Big Chill

Yes! Delhi has a number of cafes and restaurants all over, but if you plan to give Big Chill a miss, your trip will remain incomplete.

- Some say it is overrated and overpriced, but we know that their desserts are absolutely worth dying for. The pizzas and pastas too are recommended by most foodies.

4. Don't run for a metro

If you're visiting Delhi on a budget, you ought to use the metro. And if you have done a bit of research, you'll know exactly how crowded it is at times! While most Delhiites would suggest you 'push your way through' to get in or get out, we suggest that you don't. You won't just risk getting hurt, but you will also have to deal with way too many (sweaty) people around you! And that could also mean losing your moneybag or wallet to a pickpocket.

- Trust us, the Delhi metro frequency is pretty high— you'll get where you want to on time, even if you miss a few.

5. Beware of the Delhi Belly

Like we mentioned before, Delhi will tempt you into trying out the delicious street food. But while you indulge your taste buds, make sure not to overdo it or eat at the wrong places. You really don't want to return with the infamous Delhi Belly.

- Be wary of where you eat or even drink water from—no matter how hungry or thirsty you are.

6. Avoid Monsoon season

The best months to visit Delhi are November–March, especially for people who can't bear the scorching sun, dust or the water-logged roads of Delhi monsoons. Delhi winters are both pleasant and amazing, particularly in the mornings. Enjoy the morning breeze of Delhi winters with some kulhad waali chai (hot tea served in handcrafted clay cups) at The Singing Tree, an amazing tea house with a variety of teas and coffees in Chittaranjan Park area of South Delhi.

- Not every bathroom in India is equipped with toilet paper, so it's a good idea to carry some while travelling. Even though the condition of public bathrooms has improved, the ones in restaurants tend to be better options.

7. Drink bottled water

The tap water in Delhi is not fit to drink from the source, so – unless you are a guest of someone who has a water purifier – make it a rule to only drink bottled water and avoid ice in drinks at bars and restaurants. The practice will reduce your chances of feeling unwell or not enjoying your trip.

- Never take drinks from strangers, and don't leave drinks unattended. Stay away from open street food.

8. Carry a can of bug spray and pepper spray

There is no harm in staying a little cautious in the capital.

- An easy way to get rid of pests (of all sorts), both bug and pepper spray will help you stay safe in Delhi.

9. Don't book the first accommodation you find

The Paharganj area is a tried and tested option for accommodation in Delhi.

- Be sure to check out options in posh areas, like South Delhi, which offer good prices for upscale amenities.

.

10. Dress somewhat modestly

Although India accepts all types of vibrant colors, but its always advisable to remain on the safer side. Try to dress somewhat modestly while exploring the city.

- Still, make sure to be comfortable, and pick up some amazing Indian pieces from brands like Lakshita, FabIndia and Anokhi.

Except the above points there are some more points which you should keep in mind while travelling to Delhi. The number one rule to shopping and bargaining in Delhi is to known your options, so take time and see what the other vendors, just ten steps away, are offering. The sad truth remains that tourists are often exploited to a certain degree, but skilful bargaining can help save some money. (Also, the practice is fun.) Markets to bargain in are Sarojini Nagar, Janpath, Greater Kailash M Block market, and Chandni Chowk.

Delhi may not be perfect, but it is an amazing place to be. The key to a great experience in the capital is in embracing the unique, weird and exceptional city along with its people. Go with the flow, change and adapt your plans, and forget about the concept of personal space for a little while.

Chapter 10: Conclusion

As we have mentioned earlier, Delhi is overwhelming with lots and lots of stories to entertain its tourists with, therefore, you must mandatorily spend some days in Delhi in order to enjoy the true flavors of India. Live life king size with the glorious memories of the rulers in Delhi. The city of Delhi has been romanticized both in literature ad cinemas, it has given birth to ample amount of creativity in the fields of architecture, literature, music, etc, therefore, don't miss a chance to visit one of the oldest cities of India.

Printed in Great Britain
by Amazon